DINOSAUR MAZES

by DICK SMITH

SCHOOL BOOK FAIRS, INC.

Published by Willowisp Press, Inc.
401 E. Wilson Bridge Road, Worthington, Ohio 43085

Printed in the United States of America

10 9 8 7 6 5 4 3 2

ISBN 0-87406-213-6

During the time span of 70 to 200 million years ago, dinosaurs ruled the animal world. They were of all sizes and shapes. Some were fierce meat eaters and others lived on plants. They lived on land and in the water. In this book, you will find mazes made in the likenesses of these dinosaurs and similar creatures. On the left-hand page opposite each maze is the name of the dinosaur and some brief information about it. If you'd like to learn more about these fascinating animals, check your library. But first—have some fun! Go in and out where the arrows indicate. If you tape a piece of tracing paper over the maze, it can be worked more than once. Challenge a friend to beat your time. Perhaps you'd like to color the maze. (Dinosaurs were probably greens, browns or blues to blend in with their surroundings.) If you get stuck, the solution to each maze is on the following page. Good luck and enjoy yourself.

SALTOPOSUCHUS - Skeleton
All the later dinosaurs are descended
from this pre-dinosaur creature.

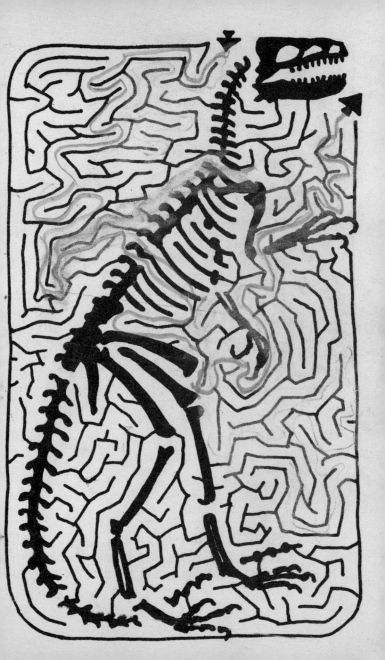

STEGOSAURUS
20 feet long ● Weighed 2 tons
Its brain was the size of a walnut.

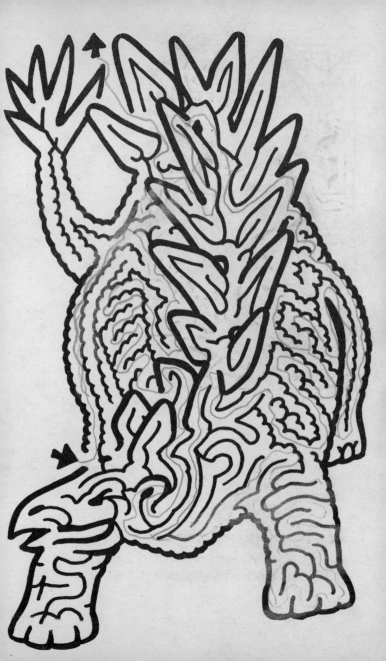

APATOSAURUS (was BRONTOSAURUS)
Plant eater ● 70 feet long
Weighed as much as 5 elephants

APATOSAURUS - Front section
15 feet high at the shoulder

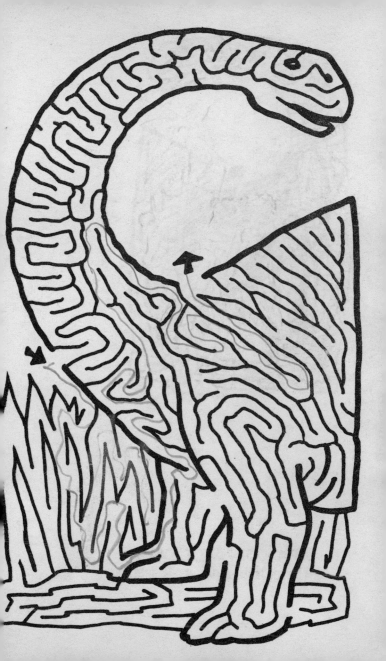

OPHIACODON
Fish eater ● 10 feet long

PACHYCEPHALOSAUR - Head
The top of the skull was several inches thick.

PTERANODON
A flying reptile ● Glided rather than flew
27 foot wingspread

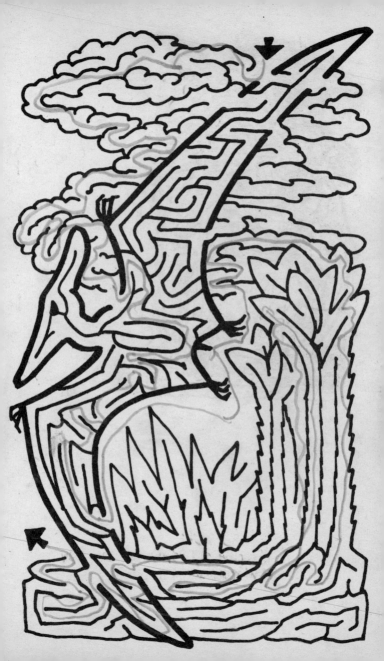

TRICERATOPS
Plant eater ● 24 feet long

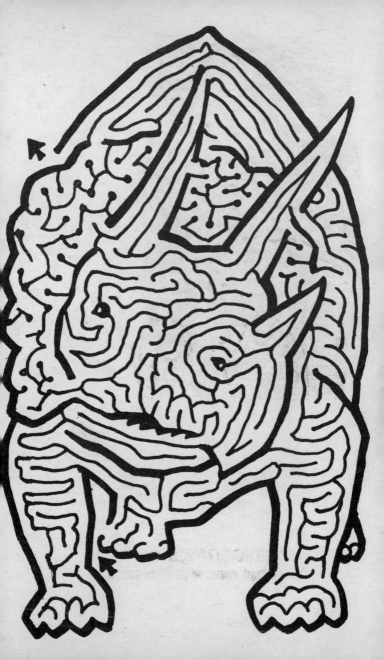

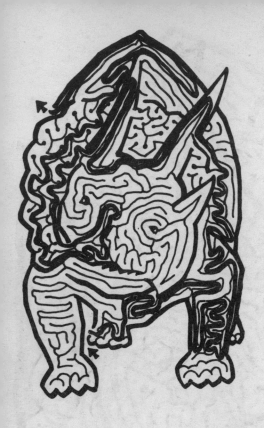

TRICERATOPS - Head
Triceratops means "three horns on face."

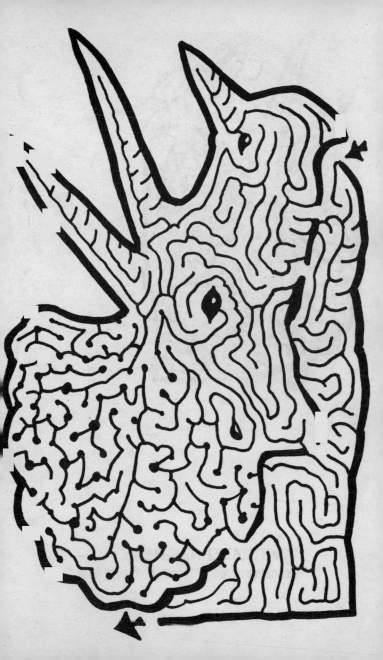

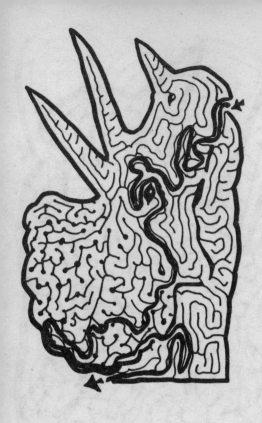

PROTOCERATOPS
Ancestor of Triceratops ● 6 feet long

KRONOSAURUS
50 feet long ● The jaws were 12 feet long.

TYRANNOSAURUS
Biggest and last of the giant meat eaters
20 feet tall ● Weighed 8 tons

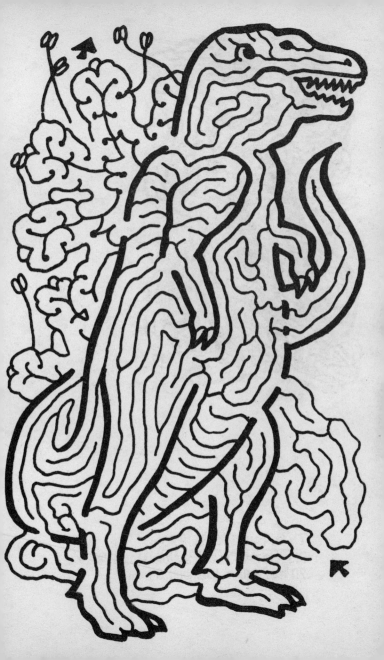

TYRANNOSAURUS - Head
Head was 5 feet long

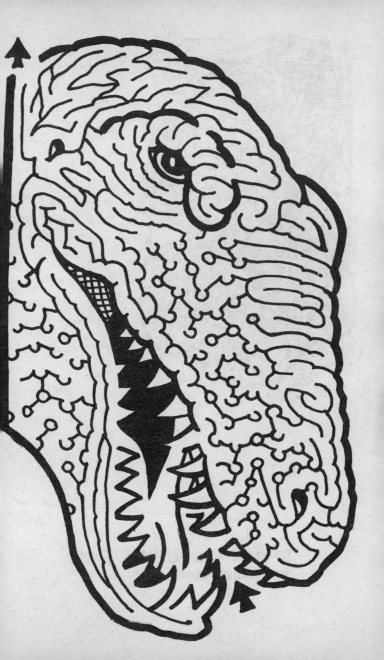

TYRANNOSAURUS - Tooth
Up to 9 inches long

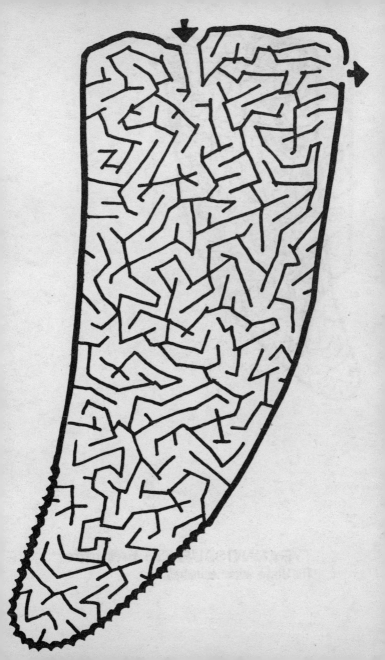

TYRANNOSAURUS - Front foot
The claws were 8 inches long.

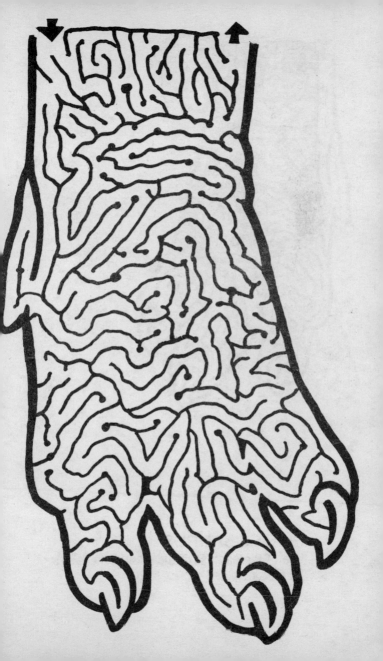

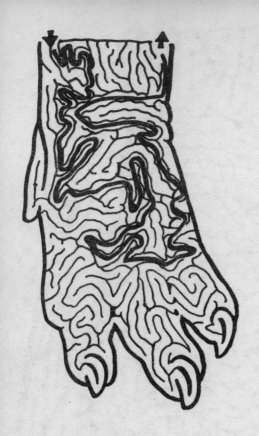

PLATEOSAURUS
One of the earliest of the giant plant eaters
20 feet long

SCAPHONYX
3 feet high at the shoulder

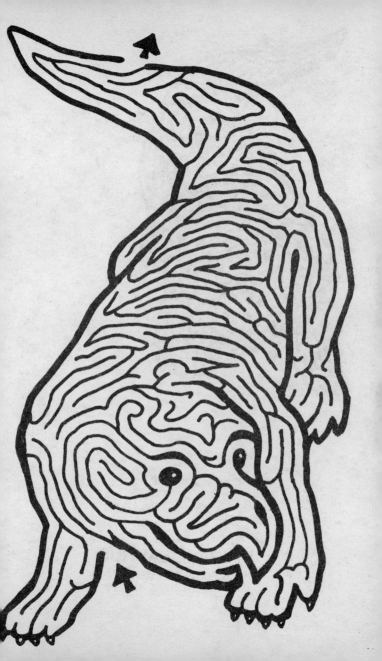

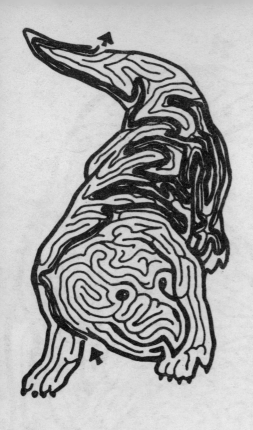

STYRACOSAURUS
Many horns on face

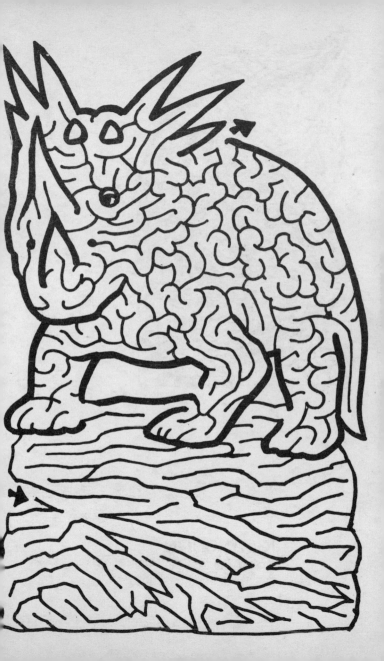

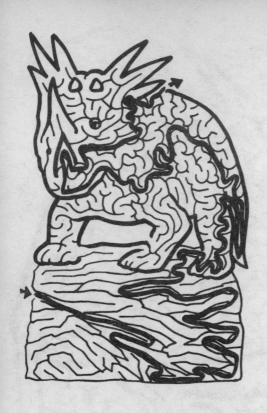

IGUANODON
One of the first dinosaurs to be
discovered and described

IGUANODON - Head
Plant eater

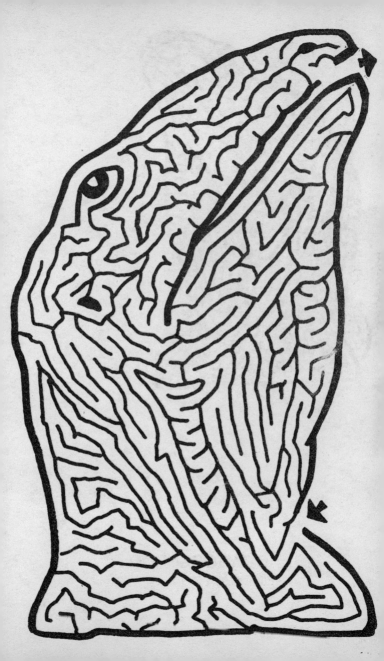

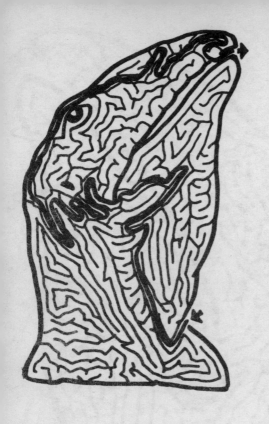

TYLOSAURUS
30 feet long

DICYNODONT
A pre-dinosaur creature

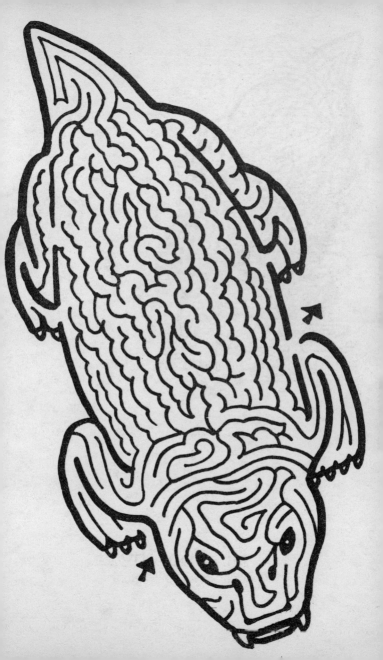

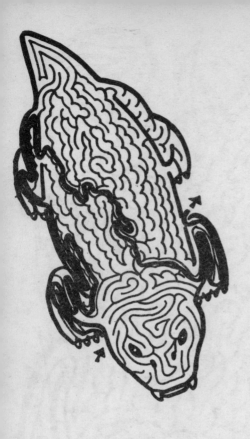

COMPSOGNATHUS
As small as a kitten

COMPSOGNATHUS-Front section
The smallest of the dinosaurs

TERATOSAURUS
20 feet long ● Meat eater

TERATOSAURUS - Head
Lived in the first dinosaur period

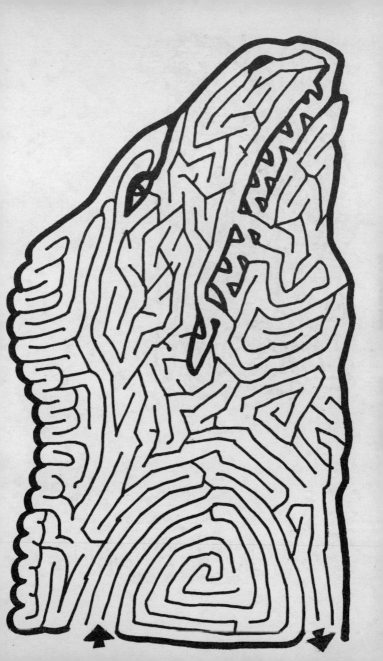

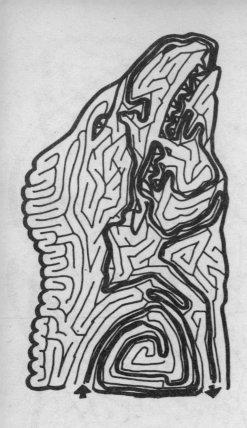

ELASMOSAUR
40 feet long ● Fish eater
Lived in shallow water

HYPSILOPHODON
5 feet long ● May have climbed trees

ANKYLOSAURUS
15 feet long ● Armored
Used tail as a weapon

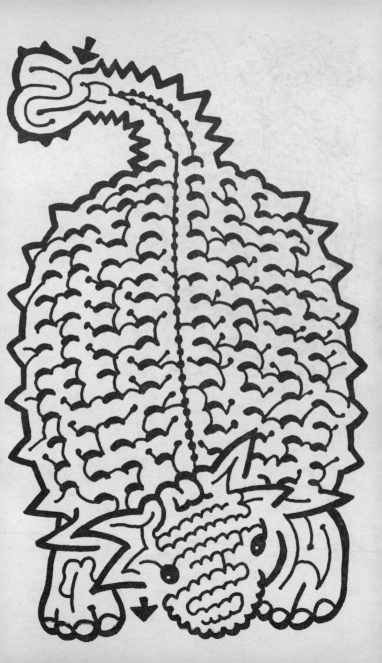

SAUROLOPHUS
Plant eater

SAUROLOPHUS - Head
Duck-billed

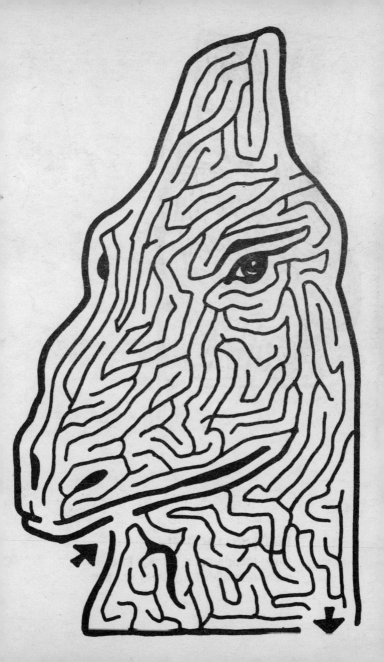

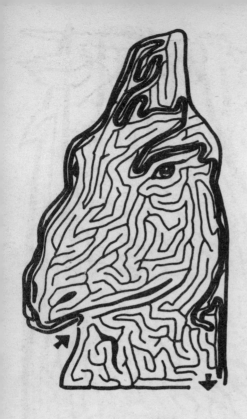

PTERODACTYLUS
Hung upside down by rear feet like
a bat and glided from this position

ARCHELON
11 feet long ● Armored

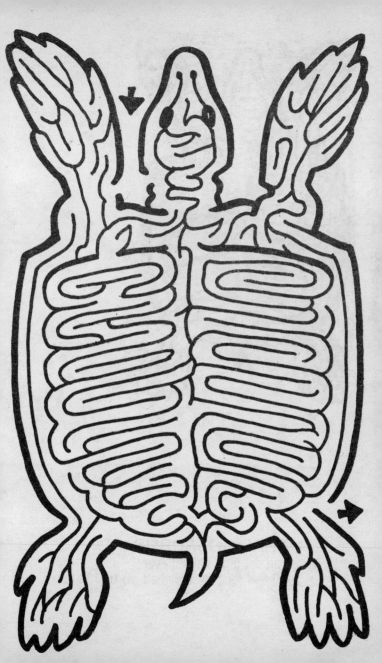

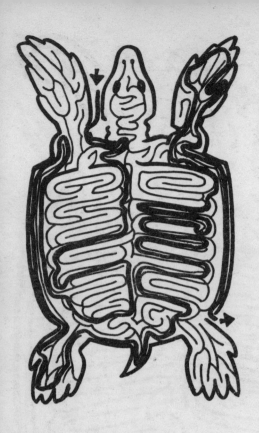

BRACHIOSAURUS
Largest land animal ever
80 feet long ● Weighed 50 to 100 tons

BRACHIOSAURUS - Thighbone
Shown with boy for size

DIMETRODON
11 feet long ● A pre-dinosaur creature

CAMPTOSAURUS
Weighed over one ton
Plant eater ● 15 feet long

ANATOSAURUS
**A good swimmer ● Plant eater
Webbed feet**

ANATOSAURUS - Head
Duck-billed ● 1000 teeth in jaws

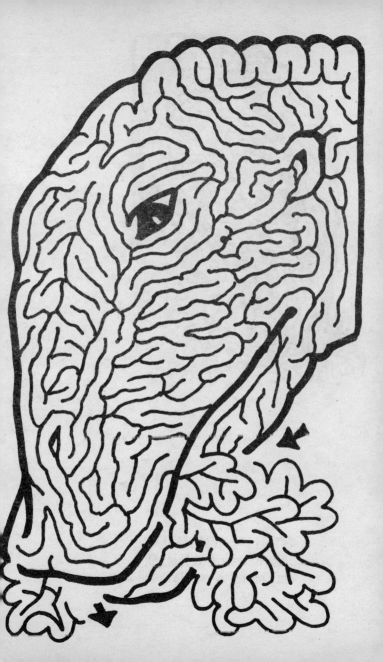

STRUTHIOMIMUS
Fast runner ● 8 feet tall
Had no teeth ● Ate small animals

SCELIDOSAURUS
15 feet long

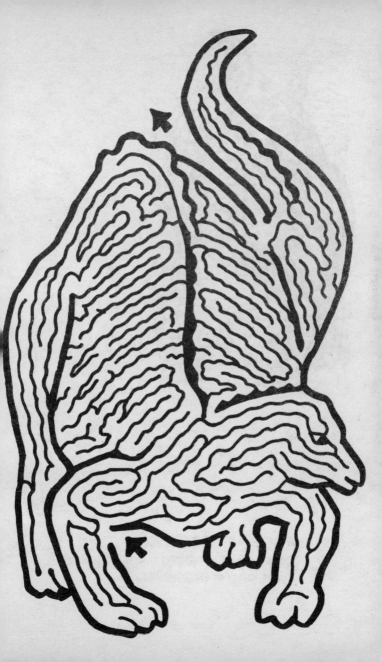

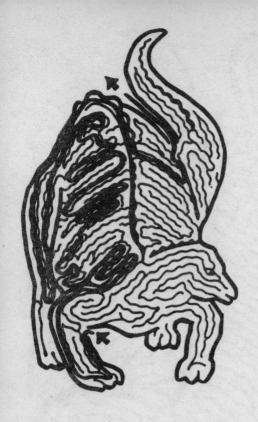

ARCHAEOPTERYX
The first bird ● Glided rather than flew
2 feet long ● Had feathers

ANTRODEMUS (was ALLOSAURUS)
A fast runner ● Meat eater
Enemy of Apatosaurus

ANTRODEMUS - Head
3 inch teeth

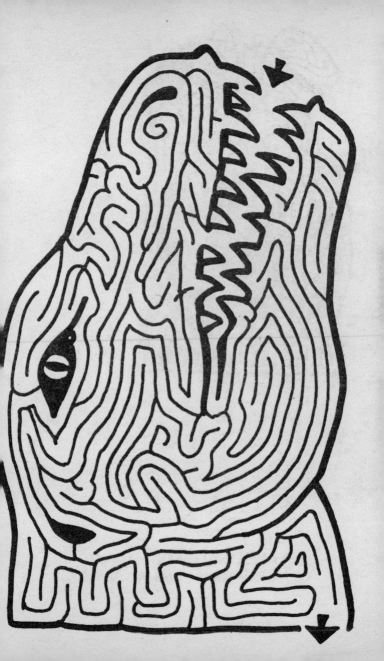

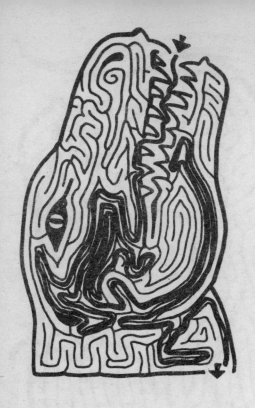

YALEOSAURUS
Ate low-growing plants ● 8 feet long

AN ICHTHYOSAUR
(One of many similar species)
8 to 30 feet long

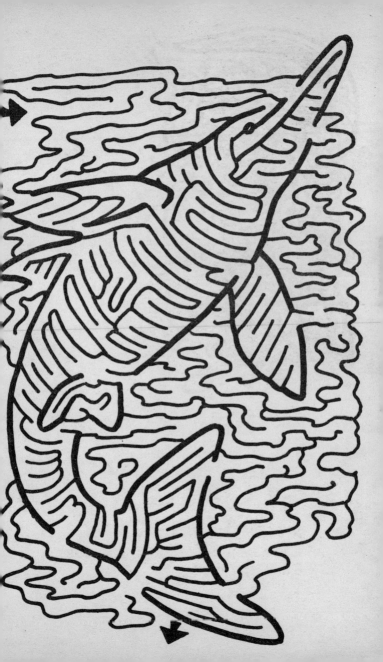